Mindful Coloring

100 mandalas and patterns to color in for peace and calm

cassandra lorius

CICO BOOKS

LONDON NEW YORK

Published in 2022 by CICO Books
An imprint of Ryland Peters & Small Ltd
341 E 116th St, New York, NY 10029

www.rylandpeters.com

10 9 8 7 6 5 4 3 2 1

Text © Cassandra Lorius 2022
Design and illustration © CICO Books 2022

Text in this book previously appeared in
Mandalas and Meditations for Everyday Living
and *Color Your Mandala*

A CIP catalog record for this book is available
from the Library of Congress.

ISBN: 978-1-80065-157-9

Printed in China

Editor: Alison Wormleighton
Illustrations: Stephen Dew and Melissa Launay

In-house editor: Jenny Dye
Senior commissioning editor: Carmel Edmonds
Senior designer: Emily Breen
Art director: Sally Powell
Creative director: Leslie Harrington
Head of production: Patricia Harrington

MIX
Paper from
responsible sources
FSC® C106563
www.fsc.org

CONTENTS

Introduction:
Mandalas as Circles of Wholeness

A mandala is a pattern that represents the whole circle of existence. Its circular shape encloses a depiction of a holistic cosmos. Mandala shapes occur in the organic world; their perfect forms can be seen in atomic structures, crystals, and flowers, as well as solar systems and wave forms.

SPIRITUAL JOURNEYS

Anthropologists have discovered that representations of mandalas have long been used in many cultures as vehicles for shamanic journeys. Navajo Indians, for example, created sand mandalas, which described journeys into the spirit realm in a similar way to the Aboriginal bark or rock paintings of dreamtime. Among the Navajo, sand paintings were completed by the medicine man, who used them in healing rituals.

Left "Looking" (see page 36) depicts the third eye. "Connecting with the Cosmos" (see page 39) invites us to identify with a holistic perspective.

Right "Dance" (see page 39) depicts Lord Shiva, who dances the world into creation.

Mandalas can be colored and meditated upon as a path to power, describing an inner journey to the center. The center is both a point of focus and the source of creation—represented in Indian mandalas as a primal dot (*bindi*) in the center. Many cultures have a tradition of using painted or made images in mandala designs during rituals to facilitate altered states of consciousness. These are used as circles of empowerment. Therefore, a wider definition of mandalas is that they exist as holistic diagrams encompassing a spiritual approach to our self-development, healing, and growth. This book and coloring block will enable you to explore mandalas for your own personal process.

TANTRA AND TANTRIC BUDDHISM

Traditional mandalas are particularly associated with tantric Hinduism and Buddhism. For millennia, Hindu tantrics used geometric designs called yantras to symbolize a spiritual understanding of reality. They are not merely representations of the transcendent realm but depict potential energies that can be processed during meditation practice. Within tantra there are also invocation practices, or mantras, which involve repeating sacred words or sounds to harmonize humans with the divine. In mystical traditions, sacred texts are read as metaphors, alluding to inner states of mind as opposed to the outer experience of reality.

WHAT IS TANTRA?

The Sanskrit word "tantra" has a multiplicity of meanings, referring to texts and practices that weave threads of connection between texts and lived experience. They also refer to rituals that enliven our energy body and incorporate it into meditation and other spiritual practices. Tantra uses our sensory experience of living in a body to facilitate transformation, rather than denying the body and its desires as so many other traditions do. In fact, a tantric perspective is that literally embodying change and living through emotional and psychic transformation of human experience provides a fast track to enlightenment.

Tantra comprises a collection of pre-Hindu traditions that are now also woven into the Vajrayana school of Tibetan Buddhism. The very different attitude to the relationship between divine and human is most clearly seen in the practice of deity visualizations. In deity practices you focus on a god or goddess whose qualities you aspire to, and imagine that their body merges with your own, in order to incorporate their divine qualities. Coloring your own deity mandala and meditating upon it is a unique way to power your personal development; see the Deity Practice mandala on page 42.

MYSTICAL MANDALAS

All mandalas depict spiritual planes of reality. Tibetan Buddhists, for example, work with mandalas to map the sacred abodes of the gods, Buddhas, *bodhisattvas* (aspiring Buddhas), and *dakinis* (skydancers), within whom infinite wisdom and compassion are manifested. Some mandalas illustrate the obstacles that have to be overcome to cultivate compassion and wisdom; these obstacles may be depicted as demons, which manifest in our lives as negative emotions. Meditating upon your journey, and allowing your demons to take form as you color, gives you food for thought about your limitations and resistance to change.

Left Detail from the *Shri Yantra* (Divine Love, see page 31).

Another lovely ritual use of mandalas is the Tibetan practice of designing and creating elaborate sand mandalas such as the Kalachakra. Part of the purpose of this esoteric ritual is to demonstrate the impermanence of our present lives and physical condition. When monks wash away the beautiful and highly intricate mandalas that have taken many days to create, they believe that this dissolves the energy created through spiritual practice and releases its merit. By mixing the sand into streams, rivers, and oceans, this merit spreads through them and benefits the world.

OUTSIDE THE EASTERN TRADITION

Mandala patterns may also be found in non-Eastern mystic traditions. They can be seen in the rose windows of cathedrals such as Chartres and Notre Dame in France, both dating from the thirteenth century, which inspire us with their beauty and transcendent power as they filter heavenly light. A rose window inspired the design of the Grace mandala shown on page 57. Through the centuries, mandalas have informed the work of mystics, such as the twelfth-century nun Hildegard of Bingen. In her illustrated book *Scivias* she published visionary mandalas depicting circles of angelic beings in celebration of God's creation. Similar rituals are found in ancient traditions. For instance, the labyrinth, a maze-like pathway that could be literally walked in order to gain power and insight, is found in many cultures around the world.

The classical labyrinth is thought to date back several thousand years, while a more complex version became popular during the Middle Ages; labyrinths still exist in the floors of many European churches. The most famous, dating back to about 1200, is at Chartres, where the walking of the labyrinth won as much spiritual merit as going on the established, church-sanctioned pilgrimage to Jerusalem. Walking the labyrinth is just one expression of a basic human need for connection and wholeness. The Hajj, the Islamic pilgrimage to Mecca, involves seven circumambulations of a central building, the Ka'ba, the holiest place in Islam. This square in the middle of a circle can be seen in mystical terms as reconciling a geometrical shape with the universal and holistic shape of the circle.

Among the Sufi orders, the Mevlevi dervishes, or whirling dervishes, use the ritual of a whirling dance as a means of prayer. Their spinning circles symbolize the elliptical orbits of planets around the sun.

JUNG AND MANDALA PAINTING

Within traditional cultures, from Navajo to Tibetan, mandalas are used to help attune man's awareness to his place in a holistic world. These indigenous traditions have been mined for decades by Western spiritual practitioners. The pioneer of this approach was the Swiss psychological explorer Carl Jung (1875–1961), who encouraged his clients to regularly paint their own mandalas. Over the course of psychotherapy, Jung noticed that his clients generated mandalas with meaningful symbols from their own unconscious—even where they had had no previous contact with traditional mandalas. Because these forms have arisen in many disparate cultures over millennia, emerging spontaneously in dreams and drawings, Jung came to the conclusion that mandalas expressed universal archetypes. He considered each individual's artwork to be a personal manifestation of a collective unconscious common to all humanity.

THE SELF AND INDIVIDUATION

Jung saw mandalas as an archetypal expression of our own personal journey to self-development. According to psychoanalysts, personal growth is the most compelling goal in life, once basic survival needs have been satisfied. Jung found mandalas an extremely potent means of self-development, and he used this method effectively with his clients, demonstrating how each person's mandalas evolved over years of work. Jung saw the

Left The Grace mandala (see page 57) is an example of sacred art based on geometry. This mandala was inspired by the intricate stained-glass designs of cathedral rose windows.

ideal world contained within a mandala as representing an integrated world and he claimed that a mandala functions as a personal guide to becoming integrated. He saw the mandala as symbolizing the perfect wholeness of the self. In *Man and his Symbols*, Jung described the practice of making a mandala as a way to integrate scattered parts of oneself, creating a center and coalescing into a unified whole around this center.

Each of us has a story that we tell about ourself—it makes up our identity. Jung believed that if our personal reality has been denied by our family and schooling or has been rejected by others (or ourself), we risk psychological disintegration. Although he believed that a human being is fundamentally self-knowing, he felt that most of us have lost touch with important parts of ourselves. Rediscovering our own story can facilitate integration and healing. By exploring the messages of our dreams and imagination, we can rediscover and reintegrate our different facets. The goal of life, according to Jung, is self-realization, which he called individuation—the process of getting to know, expressing, and making constructive relationships between the various components of the self and living in accordance with these processes. We all have a specific nature that is uniquely our own, and unless this is fulfilled through a union of our conscious and our unconscious, we may become unbalanced or ill.

If we can recognize and accept our uniqueness, we can use ourselves as a guide to embark on a process of individuation and tap into our true self. We do not have to be content with our limited horizons, but can embrace self-awareness in order to reach a higher state of consciousness. Jung believed that this journey of transformation is at the mystical heart of all religions.

Right The journey of the self. The human figure has a rainbow body, which projects into the environment.

Left The Childhood mandala (see page 49) is used for integrating aspects of the past.

THE STARTING POINT

Jung's approach is the starting point for this book. The artwork and imagery that individuals generate from their unconscious are particularly valid for that person, and the mandala forms that contemporary artists generate are also very relevant and inspiring. Melissa Launay, the principal artist, and I have developed highly personal interpretations of the theme of mandalas, freely drawing on the iconography and associations of more traditional mandalas while finding our own expression. These mandalas are offered as the starting point for your own journey of self-realization.

Right Details from mandalas on depression (see page 37) and death (see page 60) explore the shadow side of the human psyche.

Color as a Creative Pathway

When we color, we create and recreate ancient motifs that express beliefs. Even what we would consider purely decorative has meaning—simple patterns of flowers or repeating hearts affirms the beauty of an idea. Coloring connects us with nature, with ourselves, helping us give life to something in a uniquely personal way.

Color is an intrinsic part of many spiritual and esoteric traditions. It can be used in meditation and therapy: Coloring a motif helps focus the mind and encourages a connection with our selves—we can be completely "in the moment." It is a beautiful means of bringing us into our own presence, which is deeply empowering. In this state we are most creative, using our senses and intuition to create freely and bypass the part of the mind that judges or intellectualizes our work, potentially blocking our flow.

TRADITIONAL MANDALA COLORS

In traditional mandala painting, colors had clear symbolic meanings:

YELLOW, as the color of earth, symbolized rootedness, stoicism, and equanimity.

GOLD has always been considered precious, and symbolized spiritual prosperity and divinity in traditional paintings. It was also associated with longevity and eternity.

PURPLE has been valued particularly since Roman times, as it was a greatly expensive dye made from crushed murex shells from Lebanon, and was thus the prerogative of the nobility and royalty. Purple is worn by Christian officiates and associated with the crown chakra (see page 18) in the Hindu mapping of the subtle body, where it represents the goal of enlightenment.

AQUAMARINE BLUE, seen in the lapis lazuli stone which is veined with gold, was associated with a dazzling sky, evoking infinity through association with the heavens.

RED in traditional mandalas both represents and facilitates powerful rituals. It is the color of passion, transmuted through ritual actions into wisdom. It has wide cross-cultural associations with fire and blood. Red is therefore considered the color of the life force, action, and fire. Red is commonly associated with sexuality, blood, and therefore danger. Because of its association with fire, we imbue red with dynamic qualities of energy and passion. For many of us, red has full-blooded, exciting, and even aggressive connotations.

CELTIC COLORS

For the Tree of Life Mandala, the artist used non-traditional colors that give an earthy, natural feel, reminiscent of Celtic decoration.

Olive green

Emerald green

Leaf green

Deep red

Pale yellow

Right The Compassion mandala (see page 32) shows the Buddhist goddess Tara holding a lotus, a symbol of transformation.

Interpreting Color

Artists have long known that colors can create atmosphere and affect our emotions and mood. How these qualities are described is different depending on the cultural context.

Red, green, and blue have similar connotations across cultures, because of their associations with blood, vegetation, and the sky and sea. However, some colors like black and white can be subject to quite a different interpretation. For instance, the black many of us might regard negatively is also seen to represent transformation in some spiritual traditions. These traditions also value negative emotions, because they provide raw material to be transformed into spiritually evolved qualities, such as wisdom and compassion.

Whereas in Western society black is strongly associated with death, the Tibetan tradition of *nagtang* mandalas depicts red and gold deities emerging from a black background which contains all the possibilities of creation. Therefore, the Buddhist perspective on the void of infinite space is one of resting in vastness rather than fear-inducing annihilation. As a color, black absorbs all light in the spectrum. Pagans see black as protective, as it can absorb negative energy. An object doesn't reflect light that color, it absorbs light waves except for the frequency we observe as that color—so we only see an object as red or green or black because we perceive it that way, and not because redness or greenness is part of its essential nature.

Left This detail from a mandala of negative emotions evokes a tradition of positive value in emotions such as grief, anger, guilt, or jealously.

COLOR THEORY

Scientist and alchemist Isaac Newton formulated the basis of current color theory, categorizing the colors that separated out when white light was passed through a prism into the hierarchy of seven hues that is still commonly used today: red, orange, yellow, green, blue, indigo, and violet. His ideas incorporated what we would today regard as mystical thinking about the correspondence of colors to the planets and the musical scale—in which the number seven was particularly important.

Philosopher and founder of the Steiner movement, Rudolf Steiner, believed that colors had their own particular energy; yellow having a radiating movement, and blue an enclosing energy field.

Artists such as Wassily Kandinsky were preoccupied with the spiritual resonance of color. In his work *Concerning the Spiritual in Art* (1910), Kandinsky described colors as "vibrations of the soul" which could be arranged along a spectrum from warm to cold and light to dark. For instance, in mixing blue and yellow to produce green he considered that the spiritual aspect of cold blue would be imbued with the emotional warmth of yellow.

For Kandinsky, black was "a silence with no possibilities... something burnt out, like the ashes of a funeral pyre... The silence of black is the silence of death," whereas he associated white with a "harmony of silence... like many pauses in music," while violet was "sad, extinguished." Just as orange is red brought nearer to humanity by yellow, so violet is red withdrawn from humanity by blue. For Kandinsky, yellow was a color representation of "madness" or "maniacal rage."

THE PRIMARY COLORS
ACCORDING TO STEINER

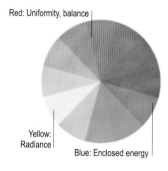

Red: Uniformity, balance

Yellow: Radiance

Blue: Enclosed energy

COLOR ASSOCIATIONS ACCORDING
TO KANDINSKY

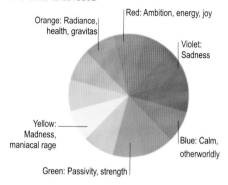

Orange: Radiance, health, gravitas

Red: Ambition, energy, joy

Violet: Sadness

Yellow: Madness, maniacal rage

Blue: Calm, otherworldly

Green: Passivity, strength

COLOR IS PERSONAL

Despite the common associations we often share about color, I think the quotations from Kandinsky on page 15 demonstrate vividly that our response to color is intensely personal.

Each of us has our own strong reactions to color, built up through cultural and personal experience. For instance, past experiences can lead us to associate specific colors with certain emotions. For Rudolf Steiner art was primarily a means of creating a bridge between the spiritual and physical world, while for Jung we have seen that it was a gateway to the unconscious. For artists, it's an expressive language for depicting your internal experience.

A COLOR-BATH MEDITATION

You can develop your unique sensitivity toward the qualities of different colors by saturating yourself in their energy—this could be standing in a green field or lying under a blue sky. It could be gazing at a screen of that color, or imagining the color.

Each individual color is a particular frequency of light wave, and a very simple meditation to experiment with your response to color is to imagine saturating your body with different colors in turn. This is what some artists do when they meditate on colors, allowing their inner awareness to guide them toward a particular palette and certain combinations of colors.

The easiest way to do this is to use the same sequence of colors described by Newton which were ascribed by the Hindus to chakras, or energy wheels in the body, starting from red at the base of your spine, and upward through orange, yellow, green, blue, indigo, and violet; see the Chakras and Color chart on page 18.

Right The Wheel of Life (see page 32) and Peace (see page 61) mandalas.

CHAKRAS AND COLOR

There are at least seven chakras on the body, situated from the base of the spine to the crown. Each chakra has an associated color. The sequence of colors, beginning with red at the base of the spine, is a useful structure to follow when meditating with colors, and chimes with our knowledge of the hues in the spectrum of light.

RED is associated with energy and the base chakra, sited at the tailbone. It is considered the home of our unawakened vital energy.

ORANGE The sacral chakra in the womb is orange, and associated with creativity.

YELLOW is the color of the solar plexus chakra and happiness, which like the sun is concerned with manifesting our creativity in the world.

GREEN The heart chakra is colored green and is associated with love, healing, and nurturing.

BLUE The throat chakra is colored blue and is associated with expressing ourselves in words.

INDIGO The chakra at the third eye is indigo and associated with vision and insight— so indigo is considered to stimulate the development of our unique vision.

VIOLET The chakra at the crown of the head is violet. It encourages a sense of bliss at our connectedness with the creative energy of the universe.

Left The body's principal chakra points from base to crown.
Opposite The Relationship mandala (see page 46).

WHAT ATTRACTS YOU TO A COLOR?

RED represents vitality, creativity, energy, and power, as well as celebration; in China, red is the color of weddings. People who love red aim to be at the center of the action. Restless and impulsive, red encourages determination and willpower. Red keeps you in the present and stimulates your senses; it has a long, slow wavelength, and fires your energy powerfully.

ORANGE is also energizing, lifting your spirit from depression to happiness. It facilitates your creative impulses, and in color therapy is reputed to help release deeper emotions underlying doubts or sadness. Orange encourages you to live with less inhibition.

If you are attracted to YELLOW, you are probably optimistic, with good communication skills. Yellow is classically associated with intellectual stimulus, and is believed to encourage self-worth.

The color GREEN balances, creating harmony and connecting us to feelings of love and care for the natural world. It also encourages growth and ideas.

BLUE is the color of truth, faith, and serenity which creates a cool and calm atmosphere.

Eternity, chastity, and devotion are some of the associations that appear in different cultures. Blue is omnipresent throughout the churches of Catholic Europe in the robes of the Virgin Mary—and sky gods such as the ancient Egyptian goddess, Nut.

INDIGO, once a rare dye made from the indigo plant, is associated with the mysterious and the profound. If you are attracted to this color, it can mean that you like to penetrate beyond surface appearances. Traditionally, indigo links to the higher mind, promoting a sense of vision.

In many spiritual traditions VIOLET is known as a very powerful color, and has strong links with creativity.

COLOR ASSOCIATIONS

RED: Energy, passion, power, spontaneity, intensity, desire

ORANGE: Creativity, pleasure

YELLOW: Optimism, confidence, personal power

GREEN: Harmony, growth, youthful vigor

BLUE: Serenity, truth, faith

DARK BLUE: Authority

PURPLE: Spirituality, royalty, mystery

PINK: Love

WHITE: Purity, immortality

BLACK: Dominance, mortality

BROWN: Grounding, earthy

GOLD: The sun, masculinity, wisdom, prosperity

SILVER: The moon, the goddess, femininity, reflection, insight, intuition

Black

Purple

Orange

Green

Pink

Red

Color Techniques

*Every artist dips his brush in his own soul,
and paints his own nature into his pictures.*

Henry Ward Beecher (1813–1887)

Let your responses to colors guide you in
choosing a palette for your mandala. Lay
out your materials, whether pastel, paints,
or pencils, and choose the colors that appeal
to you. With an open mind, wait to see what sort
of mood the color evokes in you as you work. Let the
color lead on to the next color you wish to work with.
There is no right or wrong way of approaching each mandala.

CREATING VIBRANCY

During my art degree I learnt about underpainting complementary colors to create vibrancy.
The color underneath can still be detected, and makes the top layer more alive and dynamic,
as in Monet's use of purple and orange, or Rothko's red underpainted with green.
Complementary colors sit opposite each other on the color wheel (see opposite): they
are commonly considered to be red and green, orange and blue, and yellow and purple.
Complementary colors appear vibrant because the visual processing of color in the brain
seems to be stimulated by the opposition of complementary colors in nature, as well as by
distinctions between light and dark. Tone therefore is also important. To create luminosity,
you can also undercolor with white, or build up images with white and pastel color to create
depth and brilliance. White is made up of all the colors of the spectrum, and you can work
with it to make the other colors you are working with more luminous. Working it into

primary colors gives an effect of radiating light. White occurs when the spectrum of light is seen together or when red, yellow, and blue colors are mixed; therefore everything is present within white. You can also pick out details of your mandala with golds and silvers—medieval monks decorated their holy books with gold leaf. In many cultures, gold is associated with the sun, and silver with lunar qualities. Wisdom texts are illuminated in this way.

WORKING WITH COMPLEMENTARY COLORS

The traditional color wheel shows complementary colors sitting opposite one another on the wheel: Yellow and violet, orange and blue, and red and green. Other theories link cyan with red; magenta with green, blue, and yellow. When coloring in your mandala in the coloring book, work out a color scheme before you begin, trying out different color combinations.

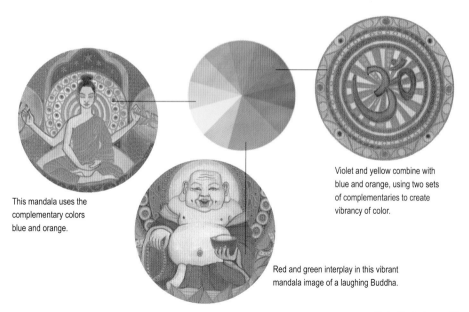

This mandala uses the complementary colors blue and orange.

Violet and yellow combine with blue and orange, using two sets of complementaries to create vibrancy of color.

Red and green interplay in this vibrant mandala image of a laughing Buddha.

Left This mandala was designed with the theme of love in mind. The artist, Melissa Launay, worked with reds, oranges, and pinks, and intensified their effect by contrasting with delicate blues.

A COLOR MEDITATION BEFORE YOU BEGIN

The circular shape of the mandala helps you to focus inward, into what is contained within the circle. In Jungian terms, the circle represents your self or your psyche. Using color to develop your mandala will allow you to go deeper into your personal experience. Colors can affect your mood and bring emotions to the surface. Look at other mandalas for inspiration, or meditate on your favorite colors before starting your mandala. You can intensify the experience by working to music that may also encourage you to go deeper within.

Right The wisdom mandala (see page 34). Practicing meditation is a way of gaining access to stillness and wisdom.

To start with a color meditation, lie down and imagine drawing the color you prefer into your body on the in-breath. Let it saturate your body as you slowly breathe out. Breathe more of that color in on the in-breath. If you don't have an immediate color preference, start with red, breathing it into your body and saturating your being. Then move on to orange, then yellow, green, blue, indigo, and violet, stopping when you feel an affinity with a color. Focus on the color and let different moods, emotions, and sensations arise, guiding you in coloring your personal mandala. Let the mandala color itself.

Mandala Symbols

Mandalas can have a multitude of symbols, depending on their cultural tradition. Here are a number of common symbols and their meaning in traditional mandala designs.

CIRCLE The universe; wholeness

CIRCLE WITH A CENTRAL POINT
The universe with its seed of creation

CIRCLE CONTAINING A SQUARE Reconciling material and spiritual dimensions

WHEEL Sacred circle with the four elements and four directions

WHEEL OF LIFE The processes of daily life

CROSS Transfiguration

SQUARE Earth, solidity

EGG Origin of the world

UPWARD-POINTING TRIANGLE Masculinity

DOWNWARD-POINTING TRIANGLE
Femininity

INFINITY Inherent balance, eternity

SPIRAL Evolution, growth

RIVER Flow

EYE Perception, vision

MOON Inspiration, intuition

Snake

STAR Six-pointed celestial attributes

VIRGIN Self-sufficient feminine power

DOVE Peace

OWL Wisdom

EAGLE Power

LION Courage

PHOENIX Rebirth

BUTTERFLY Transformation

SNAKE Circle of life; potential energy

UNICORN Potential healing

Phoenix

Snake

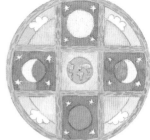

Moon

Maze

Dancing

ARROW Rays of the sun, search for knowledge, swiftness

TOTEM Animal spirits

DANCING FIGURES Joy

TREE Life, roots, continuity

MAZE Journey

LOTUS Transformation

ROSE Heart

PEACOCK FEATHER Exhibition, knowing eye

AUM Sacred Sanskrit syllable; sound of the universe

Wheel of Life

Aum

Gazing Upon Mandalas

Contemplating a mandala acts upon you in a profound way; whether you ask for this experience or not, it will happen.

Just as the content of the mandala emerges in the process of drawing or coloring it, so contemplating it acts upon you in a profound way—regardless of whether you formulate a specific intention when you sit down to look at it. Setting an intention can help you to focus on your personal journey, but Carl Jung believed that mandalas could have an almost magical power to act in a healing way upon your psyche.

FOCUSING ON YOUR MANDALA

Focus on your mandala in all its detail. Take in the beauty of the individual designs, allowing your eye to wander over its patterns and colors, becoming absorbed in the interplay of harmony or dissonance. Let the intricacies, patterns, and interplay of the different colors and other elements of the mandala draw you into it. Looking is not about judging your artistic efforts or analyzing the symbolism of the mandala, but allowing yourself to respond to what you have created and find a unique resonance for you... let thoughts or feelings arise naturally—or no thought at all.

A HEALING INFLUENCE

Jung believed that mandalas possess a "magical" significance that you are not necessarily aware of, by virtue of the potency of their symbolic content. This is what offers a healing influence to your unconscious mind. As circles are universally associated with meditation, healing, and prayer, you can work with your mandala in these ways. Enjoy!

Methods of Contemplation

Lead us from untruth to truth
Lead us from darkness to light
Lead us from death to immortality
Aum, let there be peace!
—Vedic chant

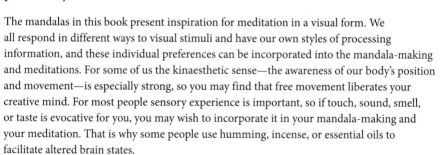

According to the singer Chloe Goodchild, meditation comes in different forms: It can come through the naked voice, the liberated body, the penetrating vision, the empty mind, the loving heart, or the ecstatic embrace—a particularly tantric means of transformation.

The mandalas in this book present inspiration for meditation in a visual form. We all respond in different ways to visual stimuli and have our own styles of processing information, and these individual preferences can be incorporated into the mandala-making and meditations. For some of us the kinaesthetic sense—the awareness of our body's position and movement—is especially strong, so you may find that free movement liberates your creative mind. For most people sensory experience is important, so if touch, sound, smell, or taste is evocative for you, you may wish to incorporate it in your mandala-making and your meditation. That is why some people use humming, incense, or essential oils to facilitate altered brain states.

WHAT DOES MEDITATION INVOLVE?

Meditation refers to an altered state of consciousness. Words used to describe states of meditation include awareness, clarity, centeredness, equanimity, calmness, fullness, love, compassion, connectedness, bliss, and light… Practicing meditation often brings profound changes within weeks—you feel calmer, centered, patient, and less anxious. Your concentration improves and you feel happier and more confident. As you become calmer, you become more focused, and more in touch with your intuitive and creative self.

WAYS TO ACCESS A MEDITATIVE STATE

The traditional method used by Buddhists is visualization. Summon up a visual scenario that feels revelant to you in your mind's eye, and see where the unfolding scenario takes you.

You may follow a meditation you know from a class or a book, or impose your own narrative. You can do this by recording a meditation so you can follow the sound of your own voice. It's important to speak slowly in order to allow yourself space to think during playback.

Consider using mandala meditations with a friend or partner, or even a small group. The relationship with others can serve to intensify or to reflect changes within.

Take a word or a theme, read the meditation, or perhaps a poem, and then reflect on it. Examine its personal relevance and meaning, and freely associate on the theme.

Use a mantra—constantly repeat a phrase or a single word, such as "compassion." Repeating the mantra pulls your awareness back to the theme you are working on.

Recall a situation that evoked particular feelings. Once you have summoned up the emotions, they can be transformed into positive feelings and directed toward other beings. The feelings are projected out universally, to everyone, regardless of your relationship with them.

The Mandalas

Here you'll find the meanings of the mandalas on the coloring sheets. There are 100 coloring pages of mandalas and variations of their designs, to allow you to experiment with different colorways, followed by 50 pages of meditative patterns and motifs to color in.

GUIDES

The helping hand is a symbol of guidance. It is reminiscent of the Khamsa, traditionally depicted as an eye in the palm of a hand. In Arabic and Jewish cultures, the Khamsa is a symbol of protection against the evil eye. This mandala celebrates the power of guides, networks, and a helping hand; as you color it or gaze upon it, consider how each word of advice has helped sustain and nurture you.

SHRI YANTRA FOR DIVINE LOVE

In Sufism, poets used the metaphor of lovers to describe the longing for union with God. The central triangular motif defines this design as the *Shri*, or "Great" *Yantra* (*yantra* is derived from Sanskrit words meaning control and liberation). Upward triangles represent the male; downward-pointing triangles symbolize the female. Feminine energy is also shown as red, and masculine energy as white. You can work with other colors to represent this dynamic relationship, or simply choose a palette that for you represents love.

COMPASSION

This mandala depicts Tara, a goddess believed to have been formed from tears of compassion, regarded by many tantric Buddhists as the savior of all. Her whole body is made of light and she holds a lotus flower, symbol of regeneration. Tara is usually white or green, but may be red, for energy; black, for power; yellow, for prosperity; or blue, for working with anger.

THE WHEEL OF LIFE

The Wheel of Life, or Wheel of Becoming, known as the Bhavachakra, is a Buddhist representation of samsara, the cycle of birth, life, and death, from which we may liberate ourselves through enlightenment. The four classical elements of Earth (the green and brown mountains), Water (the river), Fire, and Air are contained with the largest ring of the mandala. Yama, God of Death, holds the wheel to remind us that all life is transient. The cockerel at the center stands for lust; the snake, aggression; and the pig, ignorance—the three emotions that Buddhists believe need to be transformed to create a more integrated personality. This mandala is calm at its center—all the bustle and profusion of life revolves around it. Experiment with calm central colors to contain the chaos of life.

FORGIVENESS

Lack of forgiveness is one of the most corrosive of negative emotions. Forgiveness is the key to inner peace because it transforms your attitude from fear and blame into love and acceptance. In the first mandala is the Buddha, sitting in contemplation. After dealing with your demons—lack of forgiveness, intolerance, or desire for revenge—you may feel light as a feather, or experience the equanimity of an aspiring Buddha. You can visualize this Buddha above you, shining their forgiveness on you and those you need to forgive.

In the second mandala, open hands symbolize a readiness to surrender and accept happiness. Feathers are often acknowledged as a sign from the spirit, and for some, a sign of angelic presence. Lotus flowers in this mandala represent purity of intention. Try working with a palette of pale colors to create a landscape of lightness and freedom from resentment.

WISDOM

Wisdom is not merely knowledge, but a deeper level of knowing than the intellectual mind can attain. You are more likely to gain access to this dimension through stillness. Cultivate the habit of being still. Meditation is a way of cultivating stillness, and uncovering your true nature—one of calm equanimity in which the distracted busyness of the mind gradually subsides.

In the second mandala, the fish swimming toward the center point and outward to the perimeter expresses the mind's incessant flow. Like a fish which allows the water to carry it to whatever it needs, you can allow your mind to flow, trusting that what you need will come to you. The variation on the classic endless knot presents a path that has no beginning or end. In Buddhism, the endless knot expresses the infinite wisdom of Buddha. Color the pathway in the design a little at a time as a meditative exercise on opening up to wisdom.

BLISS

Delightful, intense, and enveloping, bliss is what those who are seeking peak experiences are after—an intense immersion in a fulfilling dynamism. The main obstacle is your own resistance. In Buddhist practice, meditation is used to let go of a lifelong habit of grasping things, a desire for material goods, or a need to control situations. Meditate on this mandala as you color it. Letting go of your craving for reassurance or your aversion to others can also be achieved this way.

LOVE

Love brings out the best in everyone and creates more positive energy in the world. By giving more love, you are more able to receive it. Yab-yum is the tantric term for lovers in an embrace, who sit together in ecstatic union inside the central lotus of this mandala. Together they symbolize the marriage of insight and compassion. The stars around the couple in the lotus flower symbolize guidance and spirituality. In chakra healing (see page 18), green is associated with the heart chakra, but work with any colors that resonate with love.

RELEASE

Your body becomes armored when you feel tense, anxious, or defensive. If you are hard on yourself, you may be critical of others, too. Releasing your body armoring can help you change your habitually harsh attitude to yourself and others. This mandala encourages a soft belly, where you release accumulated tension in the lower abdomen. As you color in this mandala, try drawing the air down into your abdomen, and hold your breath briefly. Imagine a ball of light and heat, like a sun sitting in your belly. Encourage the warm rays of the sun to spread through your body and diffuse outward, softening your whole being.

LOOKING

Gazing at something is considered in the East to be an active mode of engagement. That is why beauty is so important, as the quality of what you look at is thought to affect your own energy field. The third eye links with the third-eye chakra. It is located between the brows (see the face, center). Activating your third eye is believed to open you up to intuition, clairvoyance, and imagination. Gaze upon the Looking mandala, and then color in your own to spark intuition and imagination.

LAUGHTER

Laughter makes us feel good, and can be a gift to those around us. In the spirit of Laughing Buddha, Hotei, cultivate these joyful qualities by the practice of laughing. Hotei was a jolly Chinese Zen monk who lived over one thousand years ago, and is remembered for the ever-replenished sack of goodies he dispensed to all who crossed his path. His pot belly is living proof of his happiness, good luck, and plenitude. Think for a moment how your body feels whenever you laugh or smile. A joyful belly-laugh releases a wave of feel-good endorphins.

DEPRESSION

Depression can result from an accumulation of painful experiences, which ultimately overwhelm you with their negativity, blighting the possibility of interpreting your situation more positively. It can be caused by perceiving yourself as powerless in a situation, or feeling victimized by people or events. Instead of hiding behind your hands, let your hands fill with the energy and dynamism that are within you, not far below the surface. Color in this mandala as a meditation to give yourself a helping hand.

PERSONAL POWER

The center of personal power is in the *hara*, just below the navel. Meditators and martial arts practitioners develop a powerful *hara*. Working with these mandalas helps generate the energy you need to take your unique place in the world. Three is a dynamic number of creation. The trio of trees in the first mandala symbolize growth, wellbeing, and strength. The Celtic knot symbolizes a sure framework for the emerging sense of self. When you have inner certainty about the way you choose to live your life, you gain power and confidence.

The second mandala depicts the power-packed potential of the seeds of a sunflower. You can use the image of a sunflower below your navel, or visualize a golden orange-yellow light in your abdomen, glowing with warmth. Imagine this warm glow intensifying into orange and sending a green tendril down into the earth, like the stalk of the sunflower, or send a tendril of light downwards. It will grow into a strong beam of light going straight down and penetrating deep into the core of the earth. A palette of vibrant colors creates energy, helping you engage with the theme of empowerment through the mandala.

DANCE

Like the dancing Shiva in this mandala, your body is a temple, dedicated to the life force. Lord of the Dance devotees of the Hindu god Shiva say that the world was danced into existence. The familiar image of him performing this dance among the flames of the universe represents the primal creative force. Listening to music can help you visualize colors for your mandala; its quality may guide you to muted or vibrant colors.

CONNECTING WITH THE COSMOS

This mandala emphasizes the multiple connections that weave through all life forms. In mandalas, the central point or dot often represents the universe, reminding us that reality is beyond space and time. Each of us may be as insignificant as a dot of energy in the vastness of the universe, yet we all have our unique place within it. Fish represent flow in this mandala, expressing the flow of life connecting us to the source, the universe.

HEALING

Symptoms are a sign of "dis-ease" or imbalance in the body or psyche. Whatever symptoms you wish to explore, whether pain or unresolved emotional issues, bring them to mind and focus on them as you color your mandala. The lotus flower at the base chakra indicates the source of the energy that is believed to stream through the chakra system (see page 18). The colors associated with the chakra healing system are red, orange, yellow, green, blue and indigo, and violet or white.

GRATITUDE

This mandala celebrates being alive. There are so many good aspects to your life; try to give thanks for them every day. The cosmos symbolizes an awareness of the world above us; when we express gratitude, we often look to the sky as an acknowledgment of the divine. Hearts and hands express giving and receiving, in which the ultimate gift is the exchange of love. The phases of the moon indicate the cyclic nature of thankfulness; the expression of gratitude feeds positive relationships over time.

WATER

Water is associated with cleansing, the flow of our emotions, and the unconscious. In the mandalas on this page, the fish represent the flow of emotional currents. Tail to tail, they may also indicate stuck emotions—going round in circles—but also the potential for accepting the current and the ebb and flow of life.

The ocean symbolizes emotions. Emotions are part of your inner life, and many people feel they have responses to life that are as deep as the ocean. Rather like a surfer on the crest of a wave, the trick is to enjoy the thrill of feeling emotions, without getting sucked under through identifying with a particular emotion. Whether it is pride or envy, anger or sadness, malice or martyrdom, all these emotions are transient, and we can flow through them. As you color these mandalas, you may want to sit where you can hear the gentle sound of running water for inspiration.

DEITY PRACTICE

This is a lovely mandala in which you can use the image of a deity figure to evoke divine qualities, which you can then generate in yourself. We are all sacred manifestations of the divine. The heart is cracked and held by the angel, a beneficent figure who protects and heals it, just as visualizing a deity can be a useful practice to release hurt and ask for help. The roots and seeds express how this kind of deity practice encourages personal growth.

BEING OF SERVICE

Learning to put someone else's needs before your own can be a real lesson in spiritual growth. In this mandala, the heart symbolizes love in the context of service to others. The sun/petals represent solar power and its association with growth and healing. Trees support the sun/petals and heart motif, symbolizing emotional strength available to others.

PASSION

Kundalini is a libidinal energy that we might describe as lust for life. Traditionally it is represented by a snake goddess, coiled asleep around the base chakra, or energy centre, at the bottom of your spine. The energy of the base chakra is represented by fire, which is often evoked in meditations. Experience your inner fire as a wholehearted aliveness. Allow it to become a dynamic force motivating your every thought and action.

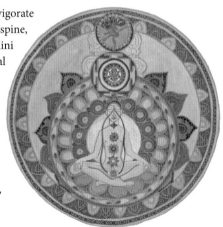

CHAKRA

Chakra techniques teach us how to purify and invigorate Kundalini, the energy center at the bottom of the spine, at the base chakra. The purpose of raising Kundalini energy is enlightenment. There are seven principal chakra points along the spine, making a network of subtle energy channels. The *Shri Yantra* of divine love (see page 31) at the seventh chakra (the crown) symbolizes divine love. A chakra meditation involves breathing deeply, imagining the energy gathered by the breath moving through each chakra in turn, visualizing each chakra's associated color: red, then orange, yellow, green, blue, indigo, and violet or white.

MASCULINITY

In tantric rituals, masculinity is represented by the *vajra*, a Sanskrit word meaning thunderbolt or diamond. Symbolized by a diamond sceptre, the *vajra*, or Tibetan *dorje*, stands for potency, action, incisiveness, power, and indestructibility. In legend it was wielded by Indra, who in Vedic times was the supreme ruler of the Hindu gods, the god of war and storms. Although powerful, he acts wisely and takes care not to harm others. The *vajra* is associated with indestructibility, and its mandala may encourage sharp, defined color.

FEMININITY

Femininity is divine, and manifests the qualities of the goddess, or the great mother. In the East, the feminine is passionate, earthy, powerful, expressive, open, giving, caring, sharing. The Hindu goddess Shakti is associated with dynamic energy. While masculinity is associated with consciousness, both are needed to manifest all of life in a holistic universe. Shakti holds four symbols of her dominion over aspects of life: The snake, drum, trident, and vase. Dynamic colors are often associated with Shakti, a goddess and metaphor for femininity.

SEXUALITY

Tantric practitioners have long known that sex can be a gateway to ecstatic experience, extending your awareness of bliss. In tantric tradition, the marriage of man and woman is represented by the image of the god Shiva and goddess Shakti in sexual union. The fruits of their divine connection rain down upon the world as nectar. In this mandala, the petals/flames beneath Shakti and Shiva are red and green, symbolizing the red fire of sexuality and femininity, and the green of the heart chakra, which is a representation of love.

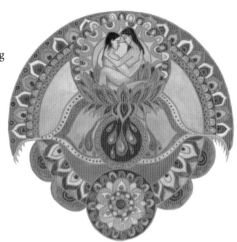

CONCEPTION

According to tantric philosophy, conception occurs when the lovers' energy bodies are revitalized by the energy of sexual ecstasy. A vortex of swirling energy rises up through the crown of the head and attracts a soul that is already waiting to be reborn. Lotus flowers, symbols of regeneration, are shown with flowing stems, linked almost umbilically to the curve of their circles. The four mandalas are mandalas in microcosm, and appear as human cells, which suggests, too, the mandala as a symbol of the microcosm as well as the universe.

RELATIONSHIP

What is key to reciprocity and connection is allowing the "otherness" of the other. The two infinity symbols show the completeness and distinctness of each person in the relationship; the figure-eight shape of the infinity symbols represents two people's never-ending love. Blue is associated with speaking the truth, and is linked with the throat center, the place of communication (see page 19). It is a reminder of the need for honesty and communication in a relationship.

GUILT

We have all made mistakes, but what matters is whether we learn from them. We need to be compassionate and forgiving toward ourselves, as well as others. Guilt is anger turned inside yourself, stemming from your conscience's views of what is right and wrong. If you have learned to act with integrity, you can let go of your self-hatred. As you color this mandala, try going through a list of regrets from the past, healing your guilt, shame or embarrassment with self-forgiveness.

SUCCESS

Success is about expressing your personality and vision of the world and following your own path in life. The labyrinth represents a journey leading to success and the expression of the self. By following the path and attaining the center, we become focused and attain acknowledged success. What you set your heart on is what you become. Allow yourself to take up more space in the world.

THE HOUNDS

Hounds were a feature of normal Celtic life. Used primarily for hunting, their affectionate and protective nature made them useful for guarding livestock and humans, and to keep as pets. This mandala represents cooperation and teamwork. It takes a dedicated effort to make a collaboration successful, but the results will be amazing.

SELF-ESTEEM

Your deeper nature is passionately engaged with life, even if you come across as shy and hesitant, but low self-esteem can hold you back and cause you to cut yourself off from others. The circle of twelve vibrant women in this mandala reminds you that you are a shining being, as valued and worthy as any other. As the female bodies taper to a point that pierces the central cell of the mandala, so self-esteem touches the center of our beings.

ABUNDANCE

The cornucopia is an ancient symbol of plenty: A horn of fruits, sea creatures, and shells, representing the abundance of nature. The mandalas on this page are about recognizing the abundance that is all around us and appreciating that we are all part of the profusion of life.

The hearts, coins, and fruit represent love, money, and health—the three things we wish for the most. Water and air represent the emotions and their release as a wish for abundance. As you color these mandalas, concentrate on what it is that you need for your life to be more fulfilled. Invite the seeds of those qualities to come into your own life. Coloring the mandala in this way is akin to preparing the soil. When you have finished the mandalas, let go and allow abundance to flow into you and all around you.

CHILDHOOD

To become more integrated and mature, many of us need to heal experiences from early childhood, turning them into lasting, character-building assets. The butterfly in the first mandala symbolizes childhood, innocence, growth, and freedom. When you gaze at these two mandalas and color them in, let them bring back some happy experiences of childhood.

Think back on your childhood experiences. How would you describe your personal qualities back then? What were your strengths and weaknesses? Did your parents appreciate you or did they try to make you change? Reflect on how you developed and worked on these qualities. You may find that the qualities that made life difficult as a child have helped you in your current life; that your own childhood has been your best teacher. Let these childhood mandalas express the colors you loved as a child to create a sense of playfulness.

SOLAR WHEEL

The solar wheel represents the sun as source of life, light, and the cycles of the seasons of the year. To the Celtic people, the sun regulated the pulse of life, its rising at dawn, setting at dusk, and its passage across the sky. The sun dictated when to reap and sow, when to prepare for winter's cold, and when to rejoice at the coming of summer's warmth. As you color in this mandala, reflect on this positive energy and carry it with you as you strive toward your goals.

THE TREE OF LIFE

Trees shade us and nourish us. They are the lungs of the Earth. With their immense fertility and longevity, they are universal sources of inspiration, and the Tree of Life has been a potent symbol in every ancient culture. It symbolizes the uniting of heaven and earth; birth, maturity, death, and rebirth; or man's place in the universe. The fruits of the Tree of Life symbolize fertility, wisdom, fruitfulness, and family. The Tree of Life is a spiritual and community symbol, an example of companionship and exchange.

SUFFERING

Suffering offers the possibility of spiritual redemption, if you can find the inner resources to transform your trials into growth. Spiritual practice involves asking yourself what lessons you need to learn for positive change.

The tree forming a central cross in the second mandala symbolizes the martyrdom that suffering can bring, but the ever-growing branches of the tree indicate growth, and a way forward out of the woods and back into the light. In very challenging or dark moments, opportunities for growth exist—indeed, without difficulty and challenges, it can be hard to sustain the effort needed to grow. The autumnal leaves symbolize the letting go of pain. Suffering can be the result of physical dysfunction or emotional pain. By accepting suffering and fully experiencing it, we may heal ourselves. Intense feelings can evoke intense colors. Working with this intensity can be a good way to express powerful feelings when you're coloring in these mandalas.

EARTH

This mandala is for you if you live more in your head than your heart or body, as it could help you to feel grounded. Many of us feel ungrounded—we are driven by hectic lifestyles and are forced to communicate through depersonalizing modern technology. Gaia is the Greek goddess of the earth who created the sky, hills, and sea. When we connect with her, it helps us feel grounded; experiencing your body as being supported by nature. Try walking outside to be inspired by the sounds, smells, and other sensations of nature. Bring what you sense into coloring your mandala, noting the colors and energy of your experience.

PAIN

Pain can feel like a tormenting demon that cuts right into you. Severe pain goes to your very essence. People who have learned pain management strategies say that ultimately you have to surrender to it. A staff and singular entwined serpent (the rod of Asclepius) and a winged staff with two serpents (the caduceus) have both been associated with healing over the centuries. They overlay a sunlike disk, in this mandala representing the healing of pain. When you color this mandala, consider the colors that express pain and meditate on those that express non-pain, or release.

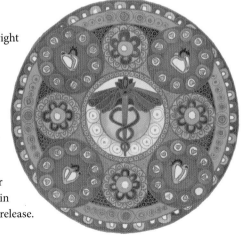

FLOW

"Flow" is a state of heightened experience that athletes, artists, and musicians may experience when they are completely absorbed in authentically expressing their creativity. Being authentic involves being true to your vision and doing whatever it is that needs to be expressed. For some this creativity could be expressed through playing a musical instrument; for others it could be through teaching, gardening, writing, singing, parenting, or meditating. It doesn't matter whether others see it as worthwhile—this is about what you want to express.

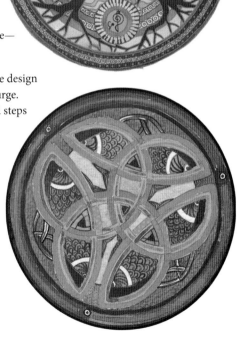

In the second mandala, the orange fish in the blue design represents the unconscious self and the creative urge. Flow happens when our judging, conscious mind steps to one side and allows our innate creativity to be expressed. The variation on the classical endless knot expresses the concept of creative flow, like the fish, and also suggests a pathway for our creative flow. The process of coloring and gazing upon mandalas helps strengthen your creative flow.

BOREDOM

Do you dare to taste your own experience and feel your power? To be free and happy, you may have to sacrifice boredom, a sign of disengagement with life. Work with these mandalas to turn your attention inward and learn to be still, to regain your inner dynamism. Boredom indicates that we have lost interest in the richness of life. The way through it is to let go of your tension and agitation, inhabit your life fully, and find your inner resources.

In the second mandala, the lizard or gecko symbolizes the self waiting to escape the enclosure of boredom. Yet the creature, like the mind and spirit, is fully animated and can leap out of the circularity of its thinking at any time. Let the lizard symbolize your boredom; transform him with color and detail, and create something of beauty and fascination. Working with a repeat motif such as those in these two mandalas allows you to focus solely on color and creating vibrancy.

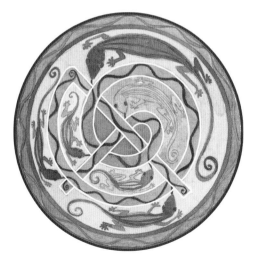

CREATIVITY

Your passport to creativity is passion—applying your energy to doing whatever moves you deeply. The closer you are to your own sources of inspiration, the more you will want to manifest that energy, and to share it with others. In the first mandala, the parrot is the symbol of Kama, the Hindu god of passion and desire. The parrot is also associated with talking and communication, so remember that the creativity process always benefits from others' input.

As you color in these mandalas, think about your sources of inspiration to provide a direct channel to creative energy. You can be creative in your style of living or you can give birth to ideas, project, or things of beauty or meaning. The most important aspect of creativity is enjoyment—we are all born with whatever produces the creativity, but it can be knocked out of us by the relentless social pressure to conform. The closer you are to your own sources of inspiration, the more you will want to manifest that energy, and to share it with others.

PLANTING THE SEED

This mandala uses the garden as a metaphor for planting seeds in your life and then nurturing the plants. Bean pods connect with roots and branches, symbolizing cosmic eggs, vessels of all life. The beech tree is associated with help, hope, and versatility.

The oak is linked with reliability, endurance, and longevity. As you color this mandala, focus on preparing the ground in your psyche. Imagine you are turning it over, feeding it with compost so that it is receptive to the seed you wish to plant.

THE MAZE

The celtic maze was both a ritual challenge and a game for the young. The ability to "thread the maze" depended on a combination of memory and coordination. It also represented the interconnectedness of all things, the multitude of life paths, and a vision of the infinite. When several choices lie before you, you may have to explore more than one before you come to a final decision. As you color in the maze, reflect upon your beliefs and convictions, and path in life.

INVOCATION

Physicists can detect sound gravitational from the universe. To us, such vibrations may only be perceptible when we turn our attention away from the incessant noise of the world around. You can tune into this inner sound—the sound of creation—through reciting "Aum." The Sanskrit word Aum has often been used to attune the individual with this cosmic hum. Reciting a mantra with Aum focuses the mind on the inspirational energy of sound, filling you with power. You may choose to work with vibrant colors for the Aum mandala to mirror the humming of the universe implicit in the mantra. Feel free to chant while you work.

GRACE

Allow the sacred to touch your life, the way a shaft of light breaks through the clouds or filters through a stained-glass window. In Hinduism, the path of grace is from the universe, through the central energy channel of the body, the *sushumna*, which translates as "the most gracious." This mandala contains the seven rainbow colors to symbolize light and sacredness. The rainbow, which we see in many stained-glass windows, is seen as God's means of communication by certain pygmy peoples.

INTEGRATION

Carl Jung believed that our main task in life is to discover and fulfill our innate potential. The goal is to integrate all the disparate aspects of the self. Jung identified four basic psychological functions—thinking, feeling, sensing, and intuition. He said that because in most people only one or two of these predominate, it is good to develop the weaker functions.

The four segments of the two mandalas on this page flow together, creating a symbol for integrating the four functions. The tiny dragonfly, moths, and butterflies in the second mandala symbolize the growth, energy, and freedom that comes with fulfilling our potential in life. As you gaze at and color in the four quadrants of the mandalas, reflect on the aspects of yourself hat remain immature—that you would like to develop.

IMPERMANENCE

Impermanence expresses the Buddhist notion that everything is constantly in flux, even planets and stars. Cultivating an acceptance of the transitory nature of our current situation helps us deal with change and loss. As symbols of change, the zodiac glyphs are used by astrologers to chart the fluctuating position of the planets in the cosmos and their relationship to one another. The twelve numbers describe the astrological houses that each zodiac sign may fall into as part of reading a birth chart. In terms of symbolism, these numbers also express broader ideas of time and the transitional nature of life.

GRIEF

You can never really lose someone close, as the good things that came out of the relationship will always stay with you. The experience of satisfying closeness has nourished you and you have incorporated it into your psyche. This mandala features the spiral as a symbol of grief. The maze acts as a symbol of the cosmos, which expresses the turns, challenges, and search for happiness, or spiritual treasure at the center. The four flowing spirals can express the different ways in which grief is experienced.

KARMA

Karma refers to actions and their inevitable consequences, in an infinite chain of causation. The snake symbolizes the complete circle of life and the impact of cause and effect. There is always a consequence to every action, whether spiritual, mental, or physical. If we speak in anger we will provoke an angry response. But if we generate loving thoughts, we are more likely to facilitate greater connection. We need to heal negative emotional habits in order to free ourselves of any destructive patterns. Working on a Karma mandala encourages us to take responsibility for the impact of our attitudes and behavior.

DEATH

An essential part of preparing for death is a review of life, looking at past joys and sorrows and saying goodbye to each experience. In tantric iconography, the god Shiva meditates in the cremation ground, whitened with ashes, where the black goddess Kali rules supreme. Kali is the goddess of death, and her necklace of skulls reminds us of our ultimate destination. In this mandala, the images of Kali and Shiva are merged as one. This mandala offers an awareness of death, which may help you to live this day as if it were your last, letting go of distractions and the weight of accumulated sorrows.

PEACE

Peace is associated with restfulness, contentment, freedom, and fulfillment. It describes a relationship of respect, justice, and goodwill. The peacock in the first mandala symbolizes compassion and peace. It is an ancient symbol, and in Hindu mythology was said to be a protector and destroyer of snakes, swallowing their venom without killing itself. The triqueta is a Celtic symbol of protection, of holding things safe.

In the second mandala, the phoenix carries the message of reconciliation. Even in the face of calamity, there is often an olive branch held out, and in the midst of trauma, individuals may be able to maintain their state of inner peace. If you are at peace with yourself you might describe yourself as feeling balanced, serene, and calm. Use these mandalas to help you to preserve your own sense of peace whenever you feel in need of it.

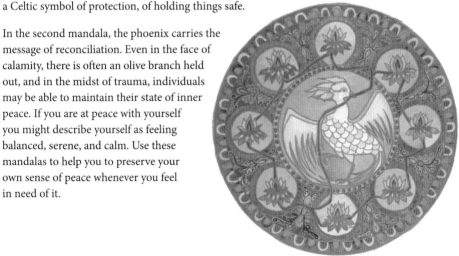

ANGER

The Buddha said that holding on to anger is like grasping a hot coal you plan to throw at someone else; you are the one who gets burned. Not knowing how to express anger, many people attempt to suppress it. However, it often eats away inside you, becoming toxic. Underneath anger are usually hurt, loneliness, fear, or grief. As you color this mandala, reflect on all these emotions as different qualities of energy. By increasing understanding, you can transform your own negative feelings into a positive energy, as well as fostering reconciliation in people locked in conflict.

AWARENESS

The Zen Buddhist Thich Nhat Hanh describes emptiness as full of everything and empty of nothing. Working with mandalas helps cultivate an awareness of this dual nature of reality, which consists of both form and emptiness. Inspired by a Celtic shield, this mandala draws your eye into its proliferating circles. Focusing on this detail will help you develop your concentration and awareness.

RITUAL

Many believe that creating rituals that affirm the sacred will encourage new, positive energies to manifest. In the first mandala, the Celtic knot is a labyrinth for you to think about your own path to wholeness.

Coloring in these two symmetrical designs can work well if you are approaching mandala-coloring as a ritual. Before you start coloring, clear any clutter and air the room. Lay out any refreshments you'll need. Prop up your chosen mandala on a book stand, and begin. Other rituals you might like to incorporate include lighting candles, working with crystals, flowers, perfumes, or essential oils, setting up altars, and chanting or dancing.

INDEX

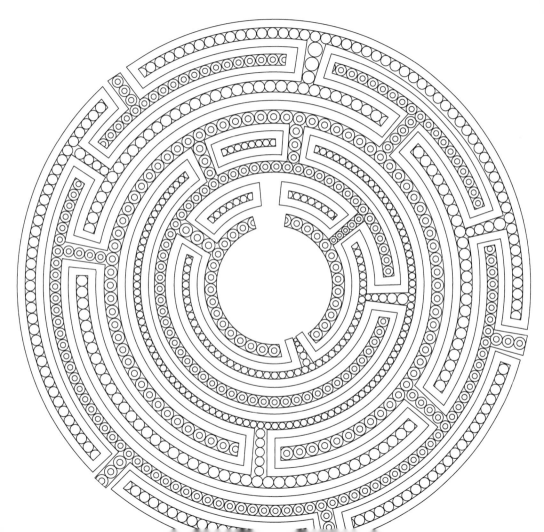

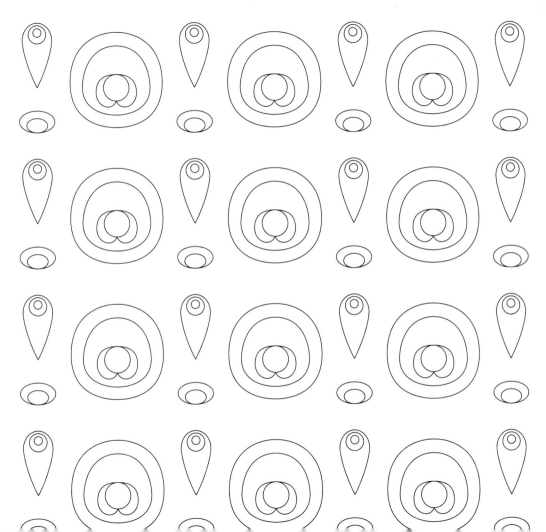

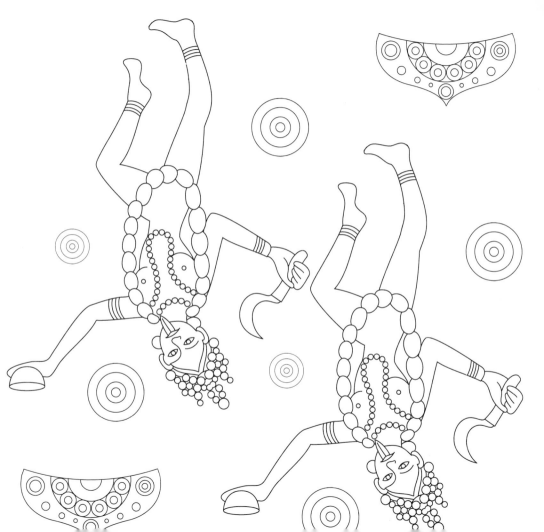

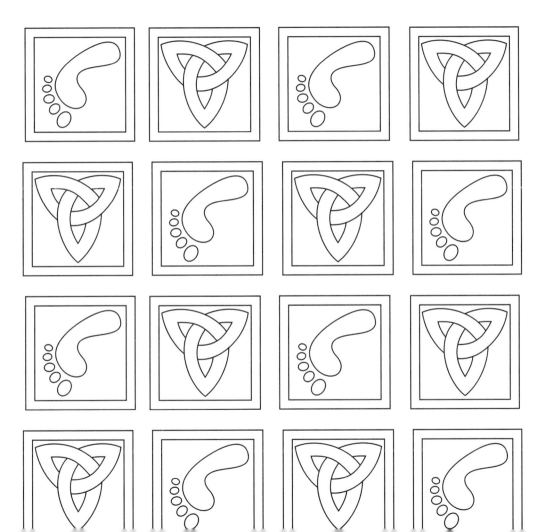

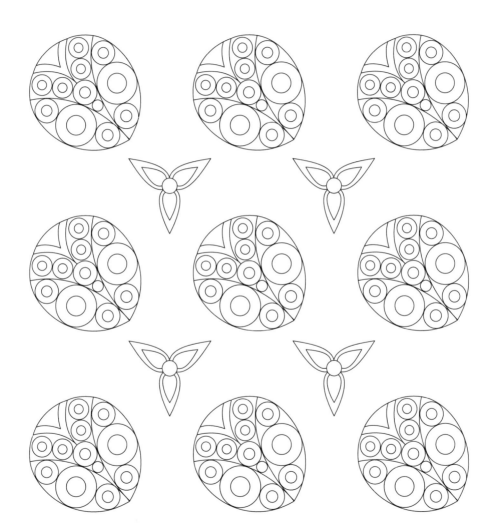

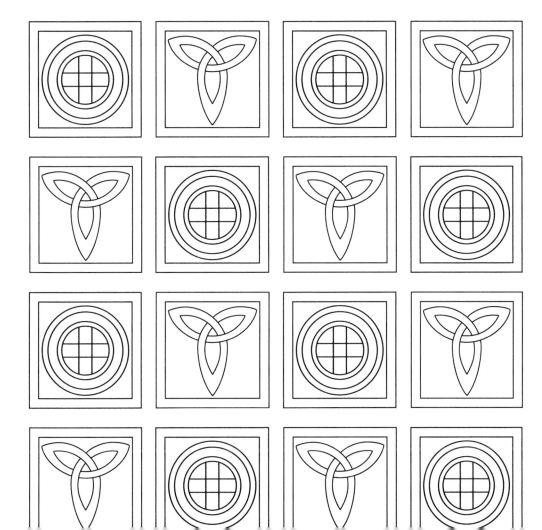

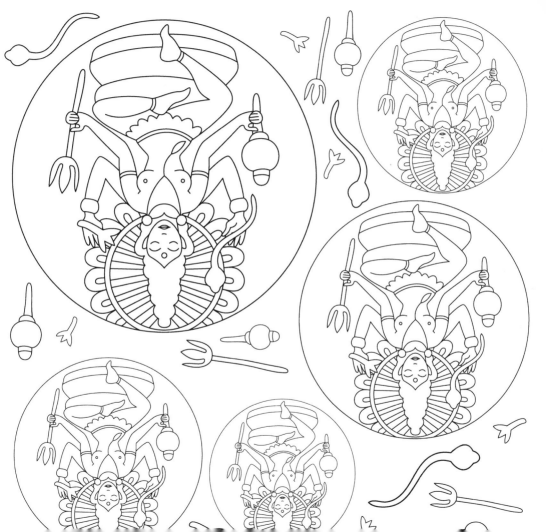

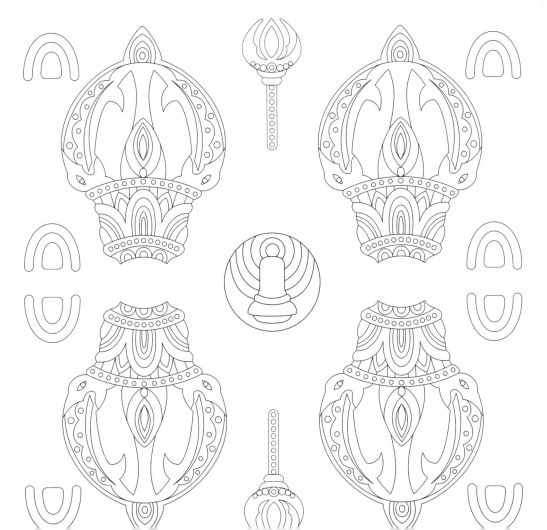

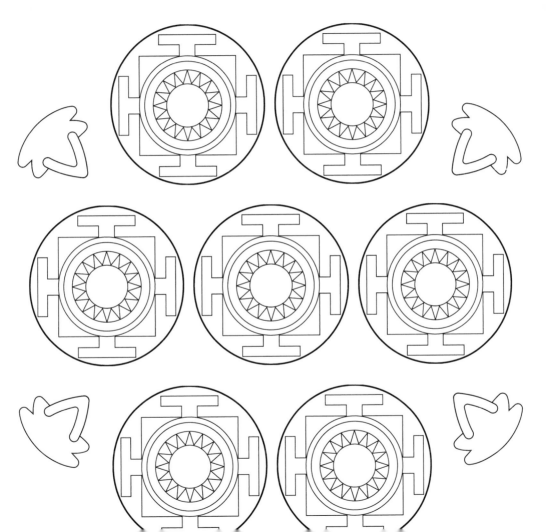

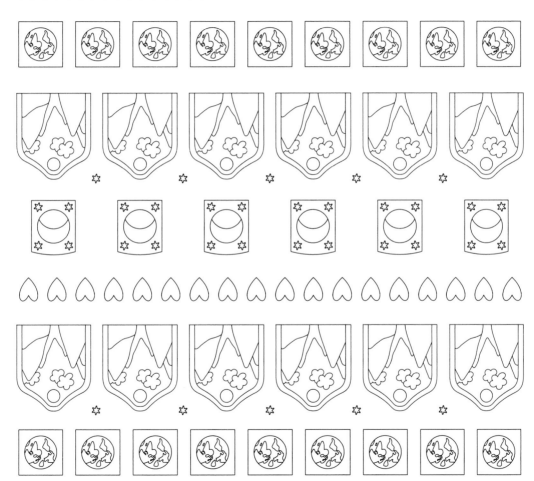

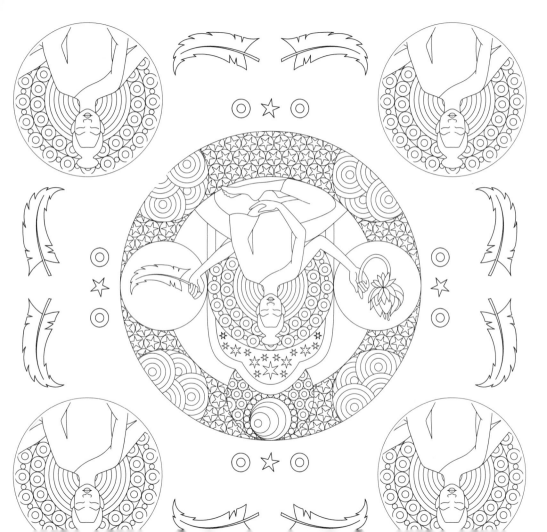

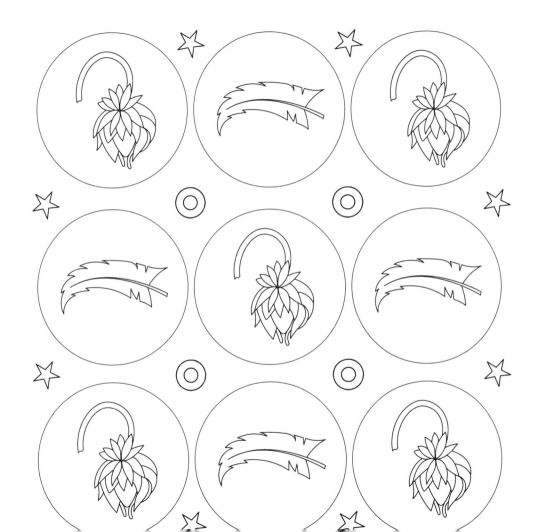